Are you a
Natural
Hatha
Yogi?

Ken Thompson

Published by
Wide Eyed Frog Publishing

End Cottage
Bilhams Hill
REEPHAM
Norfolk, NR10 4RB

Telephone: +44 (0)1603 872030

© Ken Thompson 2002

All rights reserved. Apart from fair dealing for the purposes of study, research, criticism or review, as permitted under the Copyright Design and Patents Act, 1998, no part of this publication may be reproduced, stored in a retrieval system, or transmitted in any form or by any means, electronic, electrical chemical, mechanical, photocopying, recording or otherwise without prior permission of the copyright owners. Enquiries should be addressed to the publishers.

ISBN 0-9543966-0-X

Designed and printed in England by
Barnwell's Print Ltd, Barnwell's Printing Works
Penfold Street, Aylsham, Norfolk, NR11 6ET
Telephone: +44 (0)1263 732767

Dedications *and* Acknowledgments

This book is dedicated to all the teachers and my many yoga and Alexander students, who over the last 30 years have been influential in improving my limited knowledge of human functioning and the manner in which we use ourselves in everyday activities. This process of learning is continuing and I foresee the 21st century as being an exciting time to live.

Although I am indebted to far too many people to name, I would like to thank the following individuals who have assisted in the production of this book: Reg Charlton of Auckland for providing the most wonderful scenic views from New Zealand, and also Kathy Buckner and Linda Cantrell for providing the excellent demonstrations of yoga postures. I have been unable to find the source of some of the pictures I have used in this book. If any of these photographs and/or diagrams are still within copyright I apologise to the photographers and illustrators concerned. I would like to acknowledge the skill and expertise of Barnwell's Print Ltd and in particular Karen Fuller for all the help in design and layout of this publication. Finally thanks to my publishers for having the confidence and encouragement in helping me to complete this project.

Contents

	page
Foreword	7
Introduction	8

Chapter 1

Individual tuition or a class?	11
Teachers' ability and preferences, successful yoga teachers	13
The danger of 'overdoing'	15
Ligaments for looseness, muscles for movement consciousness for coordination	16

Chapter 2

Natural ability, natural yoga	19
Your natural potential, joints	20
Ligaments and tests for natural flexibility	22
Muscles	24
Tendons	26
PNF stretching	28
Homeostasis body	29

Chapter 3

Your Body type	31
Body type questionnaire	33
Is there a Hatha Yoga body type?	37
Self-assessment profile	39

	page
Chapter 4	
Simple natural flexibility tests	*41*
Three important tests for yoga students:	
(1) Spinal	*42*
(2) Shoulders	*43*
(3) Hamstrings	*44*
Chapter 5	
Learning plateaus	*47*
Time factor	*48*
Psychological effects	*48*
14 exercise programme points	*49*
Goswami's four phases of pain	*50*
Safety factors	*51*
Chapter 6	
Competitive athletic yogi or participating yogi?	*53*
10 observational feedback points for the body in movement (yoga postures)	*56*
Chapter 7	
Who is the authority in these traditional practices?	59
Aerobic component in yoga	60
Surya Namaskar, Salute to the Sun positions	62
Beeja mantras	66
Leg stretches	69
The importance of the squat	72
Heel raising and the 'soleus pump'	73

Brief Summary   75
References   76
Bibliography   77
Index   78

Foreword

The purpose of this book is to assist students of yoga into a clearer understanding of how their body type and their anatomical and physiological make-up can be the determining factors in their potential to perform yoga postures. This understanding will be of a positive nature, not a negative one, because it will show you some sound reasons why certain things are possible and others are not. With this knowledge you will not be wasting your time trying to achieve a position which your body is unable to occupy or was never designed to do.

In later chapters we will be looking at other influences that can affect a person's ability to perform yoga practice and also looking at some joint-loosening movements that are directly related to yoga asanas.

Scenes and Sayings

To encourage a positive attitude as you read through this book, at the bottom of each page you will find an encouraging thought. I do trust that you find them inspiring, and also enjoy the photographs of scenic views.

There are two ways to slide through life: to believe everything or to doubt everything; both stop us from thinking.

Introduction

Most people who take up yoga practice do so by joining a local class. However, traditionally yoga was taught on a one-to-one basis, not in groups. You could also say that traditional yoga demanded 100% commitment over 24 hours, 7 days a week, 12 months a year, and that this commitment would of course be total, including one's diet, isolation from people, strict obedience to the guru (teacher), and therefore not something to be taken on lightly (Ref 1). The goal of traditional yoga, as laid down in the Sutras of Patanjali (Ref 2) was to reach self-realisation; this could suggest that yoga is much more a psychological than a physical science, more to do with your mind than your body.

However, what we can observe in the western countries where yoga has become more widely known and practised is that the main emphasis has been laid on the physical aspects, the postures, the breathing and the relaxation techniques.

Yoga styles also vary enormously, from teacher to teacher, from those who mainly emphasise the physical postures, to those who say that all that is required is to sit quietly in a state of meditation. Now there are a number of gurus and teachers whose styles and traditions have tended to dominate the western world. Some of these have

One meets his destiny often in the road he takes to avoid it.

resulted in a great many fixed and rigid ways of doing yoga practice. This has also meant that the teaching, understandably, has been very guru centred. Not necessarily a bad thing, particularly if the guru happens to be a psychologically well-balanced individual. However, if, for whatever reason, the guru becomes unbalanced or psychologically disturbed, then that leaves the followers in a very difficult situation.

In recent times one of the few people who has been talking sense regarding whether or not you need a guru, was the well-known educator and modern day philosopher and thinker, J. Krishnamurti. (Ref 3) Krishnamurti insists on the individual being their own guru, and that it is the content of one's consciousness and one's thinking that creates problems. He said,

'Truth is a pathless land'.

Humankind cannot come to it through any creed, through any dogma, priest or ritual, nor through any philosophical knowledge or psychological technique. The essence of his teaching is that only through a complete change of heart in the individual can there come about a change in society and so peace to the world. He believed that this radical change can take place in every individual, not gradually but instantaneously to see ourselves as we are, for it is in seeing with absolute clarity that the inward revolution takes place.

Being in tune with the infinite is being in tune with yourself.

Chapter 1
Individual Tuition or a Class?

As most people's introduction to yoga is through classes, the likelihood of getting individual and personal guidance from the teacher all the time will be small. In passing on general information, instruction on meditation, philosophy, etc., the teacher will be able to work quite well with a group of students, but when he or she begins to teach physical movements, the make-up of the group needs to be taken into consideration. For example, age, sex, motivation, disabilities, illness, accidents, etc., and endeavouring to please all ages within the group will produce some problems. The teacher could emphasise a more dynamic or vigorous approach which would obviously suit the young and fit but would soon dissuade the elderly or less able from continuing. In all physical movement systems, men and women tend to differ in their approach, so the male/female viewpoint also has to be considered. I remember talking to a female yoga teacher about the lack of men in her yoga classes. Her classes were all female, she told me, some men had joined but they did not stay long. When I had the opportunity to visit one of her classes I understood why. The whole way she taught was towards 'cosmetic' yoga: 'this one is good for your hips, ladies,' and 'this one will take the wrinkles out of your neck.' Due to her ballet dancer background, all postures were transformed into dance movements, with arms and legs moving in that graceful manner of a female dancer. No wonder the men did not stay long in her class.

*You cannot always control what goes on outside,
but you can always control what goes on inside.*

If you have a teacher who emphasises working with the less able and people with limited ability, then the more dynamic young and fit people will probably leave the class for something more suitable for them. The difficulty for the teacher when working with groups, rather than individuals, is not an easy one to resolve but there are elements to consider which may be of help.

In all group teaching, the class will tend to divide up into three groups: the first group, those who find that they are able to learn easily and have no difficulty, the middle group who are just about coping and the third group who are struggling and finding it quite difficult. Now, if the teacher can balance the programme to keep each of the three groups working within their own capabilities, then everybody will benefit from the class.

When you consider yoga practice, which postures you need to do, the ones you can do, and the ones you are told to do, etc., it is very easy to become confused. It's particularly confusing when you consult the modern day 'experts' and/or teachers, because they all have some strong opinions and advice. Unfortunately, some of their advice can be extremely conflicting and not very helpful. For example, some teachers will have a fixed routine that you do over and over again, never mind how you feel or whether it is doing you any good or not. Some will suggest standing postures first, with little or no attention to breathing, whilst with others the breathing is all important and the sequence of postures is of a secondary nature, and so on, and so on.

Action is what unites every great success.

Teachers' Ability and Preferences

Many teachers fail to recognise that their ability to perform postures, or asanas, is a gift, mainly because they have the right body type, with loose ligaments, long hamstring muscles and tendons, right leg length, etc. These attributes give them a distinct advantage over the average person in their classes. This can make it very difficult for them to appreciate the problems faced by their lesser endowed students. It can also influence the structure of their class programme, which can be biased towards postures that they like doing and not necessarily what the student requires for their progress.

Successful Yoga Teachers

Who are the successful yoga teachers?
There are a great many teachers who will show you examples of very proficient and brilliant performers from amongst their pupils. What they seldom tell you is how many pupils have passed through their hands to obtain these top performers.

I remember in the early 1970s a number of yoga teachers in London who would start off in September with a full class of 35–40 students. By Christmas the class had dropped to about 20–25 students because the teacher had made the class programme so strenuous and demanding that the older and weaker students had left! Then by Easter time the number of students would be down to 10–15 because the pace of the class continued to be beyond most people. Finally at the end of the summer term, these teachers would be left with a hard core of about 8–10 mainly young, fit, supple students, who thrived on this

Knowledge is the root of success.

type of yoga. So a teacher can obtain the pupils they want by the way they structure their class. This principle will of course apply to all students learning any other skills.

Most noticeable progress in learning so-called 'physical' skills is in the first six months to a year. A skilled coach can soon pick out the 'natural' performer in this time. By 'natural' I mean those people who have got it all going for them in that particular skill, that is, they find it all comes so easily to them without really having to struggle. We have all come across those 'natural' swimmers, runners, dancers and you should remember that there are 'natural' Hatha yogis too.

A truly successful yoga teacher is one who can inspire all students to progress and achieve, irrespective of their limitations. After all, in most class learning situations there will always be those three distinct groups to consider: the students who find that learning comes easily to them, then the students who are struggling and finding it very difficult and, finally, the middle group who are just able to cope. Now, obviously, if the teacher emphasises the top group and pushes ahead with the more difficult aspects of the skill, the strugglers and some of the middle group are going to leave. However, if the tutor focuses on those at the bottom, those at the top are going to get bored and leave. To be able to stimulate everyone in the class is where the clever and experienced teacher comes into their own. These teachers are rather rare, they have normally been teaching for a good many years and know a great deal about human nature. They know how to have an adaptable and flexible approach to their subject and they are not frightened to try out new ideas or discard old ways which no longer work. The following saying applies to them:

'Teaching means learning the rules, experience means learning the exceptions.'

The ancestor of every action is thought.

The Danger of 'Overdoing'

Please remember that when you stretch your body, as well as stretching muscles, connective tissue, tendons, ligaments, you are also going to be stretching your nerves. 'Now, not a lot of people know that,' as Michael Caine would say!

We all know that if you overstretch beyond your natural limit you risk tearing muscle fibre, tendons, ligaments, etc. However, what is not so obvious is that you will be stretching your nervous system. One of the results of this is that you can become 'highly strung'; this is noticeable in dancers who have pushed themselves to achieving more advanced and strenuous positions. This can also happen in yoga, particularly to yoga teachers who are fanatical in their approach to the postures and spend many hours every day pushing their bodies to further and further limits, to gain what? Remember there will always be someone out there who can go further, mainly because they are 'naturally built' to do so.

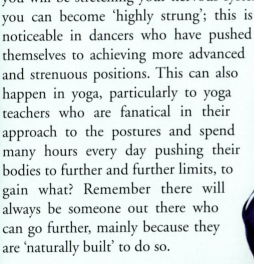

Detached from the senses, you are free.

Ligaments for Looseness,
Muscles for Movements,
Consciousness for Coordination

Ligaments account for 47% of human flexibility and, as most ligaments are not designed to stretch, those people who are born with loose ligaments will always have the edge over their tight ligamented friends. Of course, it is possible during a person's formative years to stretch ligaments. This does happen in circus families, in dance academies, or gymnastic clubs where small children are pushed into achieving extreme positions. During this early part of a child's development, when everything is growing, it is possible to stretch ligaments. However, if this stretching is taken too far, it may set up problems that do not surface until much later in life.

Once adult development is achieved, the stretching of ligaments is not possible, except for some ligaments like those in the spine, which are made of a yellow elastic tissue and these do allow movement.

Muscles, of course, can be stretched but remember that muscles only account for 41% of the body's flexibility. Muscles are attached to the bone directly or through tendons, which are a continuation of the muscle spindles. The two ends of a muscle are referred to as origins and insertions. In general, when a muscle contracts and shortens its length, the insertion end is drawn towards the origin. However, some muscles, like the rectus abdominous, have a reverse origin and insertion depending on the way in which the body is moved.

Vitality and beauty are gifts of nature for those who live according to its laws.

Most people tend to overdo all their muscular movements, whether by putting more effort into their everyday actions, or through any exercise system that they decide to follow.

This overuse of energy is of course not intentional, it has simply become an habitual response to a stimulus or stimuli. Muscular movement is controlled by the nervous system. So, when we learn most muscular skills, it means programming a 'muscle memory' or a piece of 'software' on to our 'hard disc' or lower brain (cerebellum).

You can begin to see that developing a programme for each yoga student is very much an individual matter and really requires the traditional guru/chela relationship, so that corrections and adjustments can be made quickly before bad habits or injuries become established.

Unfortunately most yoga students in western countries learn their yoga in groups or classes. The teacher is obviously handicapped through this because with the best will in the world they are unable to keep their eye on everybody at once. The responsibility therefore comes back to the individual student to use their own common sense and judgement as to what is possible, and what is not, and the wisdom to know the difference.

One way to observe the accomplished master is always to look at the face of the yoga practitioner as well as the posture being performed: any sign of discomfort will show up very quickly on the face.

I accept perfect health as the natural state of being.

Patience and diligence, like faith, remove mountains.

Chapter 2
Natural Ability?

1. What do we mean by 'natural ability'?
2. Observing the 'natural' swimmer, runner, singer, dancer, musician, sports person, etc.
3. What is the percentage of 'naturals' to average in different activities– 1%, 5%?
4. Do we all have a 'natural' ability to perform some skill or activity well?
5. What criteria do we use for making a judgement on the 'natural' ability of an individual?

These are some of the questions we need to be asking, to discover more about natural ability.

Natural yoga

Exactly what do we mean by the word 'natural'? If we look in the dictionary we find under 'natural':

'Normal, conformable to the ordinary course of nature, not exceptional or miraculous or irregular. Existing in or by nature, not artificial, innate, inherent, self-sown, uncultivated, lifelike; unaffected, easy-mannered, not disfigured or disguised. <u>Not surprising, to be expected, destined to be such by nature.</u>'

Now what is normal, or natural, for one person may not be so for another. Also what may be natural, or normal, for someone at 5 years of age, may not be so at 25 years, or later at 55, and certainly not at 85.

It's what you learn yourself, not what others teach you, that really matters.

Whenever you start to make comparisons between different age groups, there will always be large variations in areas such as strength, flexibility, and co-ordination. However, although a natural decline in ability is expected as you get older, if you are gifted with natural flexibility, strength, etc., it is possible that you can maintain those gifts for a longer time through your life with regular practice.

'Natural' yoga should be something that is 'not surprising, to be expected'. One should see this in the performance of postures. The student should be working well within their natural capacity, not subjecting themselves to any stress or strain or a great deal of undue effort but instead moving in a graceful and controlled manner. Also add to this the subtle differences in physical performance between male and female.

Your Natural Potential
Joints

A joint, or articulation, is formed by the meeting of two or more bones. A joint can be immovable, slightly movable or freely movable. In movable joints the two bone ends are covered with cartilage and connected by a fibrous capsule. The capsule is lined with smooth tissue called synovial membrane which secretes a fluid to lubricate the joint. A joint with a wide range of movement, such as the shoulder joint, has fewer ligaments than the hip joint which is less mobile but which is adapted to bearing more body weight.

The more one knows, the more one simplifies.

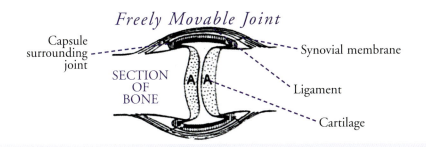

Freely Movable Joint

There are six types of freely movable joints

1. Gliding joint. Flat surfaces are in contact. Examples are the joints between the articular processes of adjacent vertebrae and between the bones of the tarsus.

2. Hinge joint. Allows movement in one plane only, at right angles to its transverse axis. Examples are the elbow, knee and ankle joints, and the joints of the fingers and toes.

3. Pivot joint. A pivot-like process, held within a fibrous ring, rotates about its long axis. Examples are the joint between the upper ends of radius and ulna and between the atlas and the vertical process of the axis.

4. Condyloid joint. A convex elliptical articular surface fits into a concave articular surface. An example is the wrist which allows movements in all directions but no rotation round the central axis.

5. Saddle joint. The surfaces allow concavo-convex movement similar to a condyloid joint. An example is the carpo-metacarpal joint of the thumb.

6. Ball and socket joint. Movement in any direction as well as rotation round the central axis. Examples are the hip and shoulder joints.

May each find what he seeks.

Ligaments
Contribute 47% of human flexibility

An observation that I have made over a long period of time is that big-boned people, that is the meso/endomorph somatotype, seem to be looser and freer in their movements than other body types. This could be because of the larger surface area of their joints but is more likely to be related to loose ligaments. Ligaments bind bone to bone; they are composed mainly of bundles of collagenous fibres which are placed parallel to or closely interlaced with each other. They are pliant and flexible so as to allow perfect freedom of movement but are strong, tough, and inextensible so as not readily to yield to applied forces. Although not generally designed to stretch, some ligaments consist entirely of yellow elastic tissue; these are to be found in the spine connecting the laminae of adjacent vertebrae.

Some people seem to have very loose ligaments. They are there right from birth and stay with them throughout their lives. Even with the natural tightening up that is inevitable with age, they will always have the edge over their tight ligamented friends. Let's have a look at some loose ligament tests.

Fingers: Bring hands together, then lift palms away as far as you can whilst keeping the fingers still touching. The distance your palms move away will indicate the looseness of your joints: (a) slightly away, tight; (b) palms 45° away, average; (c) palms 90° away, loose joints. See picture left.

Stillness is stagnation and death, movement is life.

Ligament looseness in one part of the body does not necessarily mean it exists all over. However, if you examine several joints around the body you can begin to build up a picture of that person's general flexibility. After checking the fingers take a look at the thumb: here is a simple test that is widely known.

Thumb joint test: Try bending the thumb back to touch the forearm, using your other hand to do so. Touching the arm would indicate a loose joint. See example to the right.

Some people with exceptionally loose ligaments may be able to try the following thumb test below right.

Elbow joint test: Straighten one arm against a wall or the floor and lock out your elbow joint. Is the arm straight or does it hyperextend? See example below.

Freedom and clarity of mind must be in the now.

Muscles
Contribute 41% of human flexibility

There are 215 pairs of muscles in the body. Some are referred to as support or anti-gravity muscles. These are mainly red fibre, or slow twitch, they are generally deep-lying muscles and their basic job is to keep the body upright.

The simplest form of muscle action is contraction, by which the points of origin and insertion are drawn towards each other. This type of muscle work is called concentric. For example, when picking up an object, the muscles that flex the elbow are doing the work. Static work is done when the muscles do not shorten or lengthen visibly when holding an object steady in your hand. Eccentric work is done when muscles extend and give in to resistance, e.g. when the object is lowered.

The striped or voluntary muscles rarely act alone.
The prime mover (agonist) is the major muscle initiating a movement.
The antagonist muscle wholly opposes the prime mover, it also relaxes reciprocally through the process of reciprocal inhibition.
A synergist is where a muscle teams up with another muscle to produce movement which neither could perform alone.
A stabiliser muscle provides a controlled steady base from which a prime mover can act. Voluntary muscles when contracting and moving the body produce an isotonic action. When the muscle contracts but there is no movement, that is an isometric action.

There are many instances in the body where a muscle acts upon more than one joint.

Postive thoughts keep you in tune with the universe.

A muscle, for example, can produce a movement of flexion in each of the joints over which it passes or it may produce flexion in one joint and extension in another. The two types of movement may be produced simultaneously or separately. For example, the long tendons which flex the fingers pass over several joints, producing in each one the same type of movement, namely flexion. The quadriceps muscle, however, a part of which originates from the front of the hip bone, can flex the hip and extend the knee. In walking or running, it is performing both movements: when the knee joint is held fixed, it flexes the hip - if the hip joint is fixed, it extends the knee.

Three important points to remember.

1. A contracted muscle shortens its length and a relaxed muscle will regain its length.
2. So if you wish to stretch a muscle, the best thing to do is to relax and then stretch.
3. Yet most people approach stretching by doing the opposite, that is trying too hard.

One way to overcome the limitation you were born with is to start practising from an early age. So that, if for example during your formative years (say 5–15 years) you were trained in ballet, gymnastics, acrobatics or contortion, you could find that it is possible to stretch ligaments and muscles beyond their natural limits. See picture at the top of the page. This does happen for a number of girls and boys in ballet classes. Unfortunately, some of the stretching can cause problems in later life, as with the iliofemoral and pubofemoral ligaments which have to be loose to achieve a good turn out of the legs. This has resulted in lower back problems for dancers as they get older.

A similar problem happens to yoga students who overstretch themselves in practice but do not suffer the effects till later on in life.

Every experience is a success.

Tendons
Contribute 10% of human flexibility

Muscles of course can be stretched but tendons are not designed to, their purpose is to anchor the muscle to a bone.

The extremities of each muscle are attached to the bone or other structures, either by bands of strong white fibrous tissue called tendons or by direct attachment of muscle fibres. As a general rule, the end of the muscle nearer the trunk is attached either by its muscle fibres or by a short tendon, whereas the end further away from the trunk is more often attached by a tendon which is of greater length. Tendons enable muscles to act from a distance, for example, the long tendons of the muscles of the forearm, which bend the fingers. The mass of muscle is thus closer to the source of its blood supply and away from the fingers whose mobility it would hinder.

The tendon jerk
When the muscle belly is suddenly stretched, as occurs with a tendon tap, the sensory endings of the muscle spindle are also stretched. This information is relayed by the fast afferent neuron to the motor neuron pool, where it synapses with an alpha motor neuron. An impulse is then relayed to the extrafusal muscle fibres of that motor unit, which in turn contract, thereby off-loading the stretch on the spindle so its activity ceases. If the tendon jerk was all that happened in response to stretch, maintaining or changing one's posture would be awkward because the spindle would be undergoing regular unloading when the muscle contracts. Unlike the momentary stimulus applied in the tendon jerk, the 'stretching' effect of gravity on the muscles is always present.

Blessed is he who expects nothing for he shall never be disappointed.

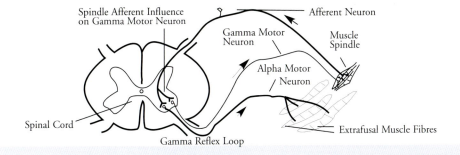

Reciprocal inhibition

When an afferent neuron from an activated muscle spindle enters the spinal cord it also synapses with an inhibitory interneuron. This inhibitory neuron in turn synapses with the alpha motor neuron of the antagonist muscle, causing that muscle to relax, thereby allowing the original prime mover to produce the movement required.

GTO - *Golgi tendon organ*

Golgi tendon organs, like muscle spindles, are sensory receptors lying in muscles. They are placed along the musculo-tendinus interfaces, as well as in the tendons themselves. Golgi tendon organs fire when excessive tension, either by contraction or elongation, is placed on the tendon. When this happens, an inhibitory impulse is sent to the muscle causing it to relax, thereby removing the excessive tension. This is called autogenic inhibition, or the inverse myotatic reflex.

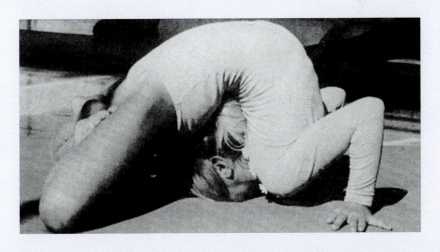

A journey across the world begins with one step.

PNF - *proprioceptive neuromuscular facilitating*

The PNF method was developed as a physical therapy procedure for the rehabilitation of patients, to help restore a full range of joint movement and to lengthen and strengthen muscles.

The PNF procedure has been used as a way of increasing flexibility in athletes since the 1970s and has now been taken up by yoga students. This technique is based on the 'stretch reflex' action, which causes the muscle to contract and the GTO action which asks the muscle to relax. Contracting a muscle that has been stretched activates the GTO, which causes the muscle to relax, thereby enabling further stretching to take place. There are a number of ways of applying the PNF technique to stretch muscles. You could use gravity and body weight or a practice partner if available.

One of the most useful ways to apply a passive stretch is to contract (isometrically) the muscle being stretched for around six seconds, then relax the muscle completely for one or two seconds. By applying a passive stretch once more, the muscle will normally increase in length. This method is sometimes called the contraction-relaxation-stretching, or passive PNF method.

Another way is to take a movement as far as possible through active muscle work for six seconds, then a six-second maximum isometric muscle contraction of the stretched muscles, perhaps by using a practice partner, then to try to move further with active muscle work. This is sometimes called active PNF.

They can because they think they can.

Homeostasis Body

The coordination of human movement patterns is a skill which we all have to learn: no baby is born walking! We all have to go through a trial and error process before we achieve a satisfactory result.

On the other hand, we have a good many automatic actions, like the stretch reflex response in muscles and the support reflexes that activate the so-called 'anti-gravity' muscles. These muscles are mainly red fibre or 'non-fatigue' support muscles, some of which are situated deep in the back alongside the spine and in the legs; their main job is to keep us upright.

The human body also works on a 'homeostasis' basis, that is, the body's own intelligence is always trying to maintain a balance between the many different physiological functional systems, thus maintaining the body's working integrity.

Please also remember that the body is:

1. Self healing,
2. Self adjusting,
3. Self renewing,
4. Self regulating,
5. Harmony and balance, this is our natural state.

The human body is also able to adapt to outside environmental issues, like noise, pollution, over-crowding, etc., although sometimes at a price.

Posture becomes perfect when effort to that end ceases.

The skeleton, indicating the major joints

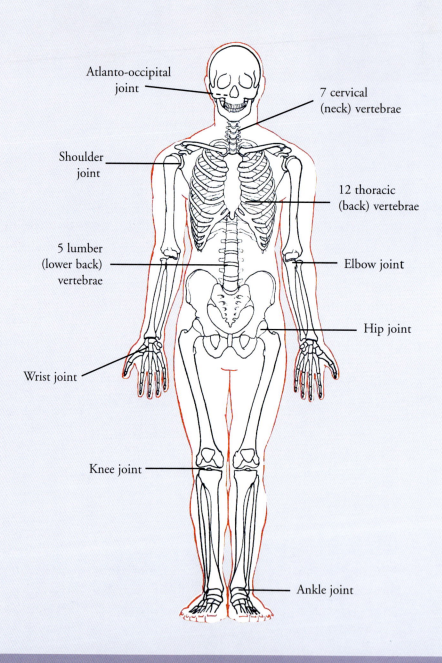

'Tis the mind that makes the body rich.

Chapter 3
Your Body Type

It is widely believed that different body types prefer different kinds of exercise. The most extensively employed method for classifying body types is known as somatotyping. This technique originated with the work of W. H. Sheldon and his associates in America in the 1940s (Ref 5).

Somatotyping defines physiques as endomorph (big boned inclined to be fat), mesomorph (muscular, athletic) and ectomorph (small boned, thin). These component names are derived from the three original layers of the human embryo. A subjective score is credited to each of these elements on a seven-point scale and the somatotype is recorded as a three-figure number. The three components in the somatotype rating relate to fat, muscle and bone. The figure one represents the lowest and seven the highest, so we have the following which would represent the three extremes: endo, meso and ectomorph:

	Endomorph	Mesomorph	Ectomorph
Fat	7	1	1
Muscle	1	7	1
Bone	1	1	7

On the next page is a somatotype chart, extreme mesomorph at the top, extreme ectomorph bottom right-hand corner and extreme endomorph bottom left-hand corner. The extreme body type is rare. In the general population the 452 is a relatively common somatotype.

If anything is sacred the human body is sacred.

Somatotype Chart

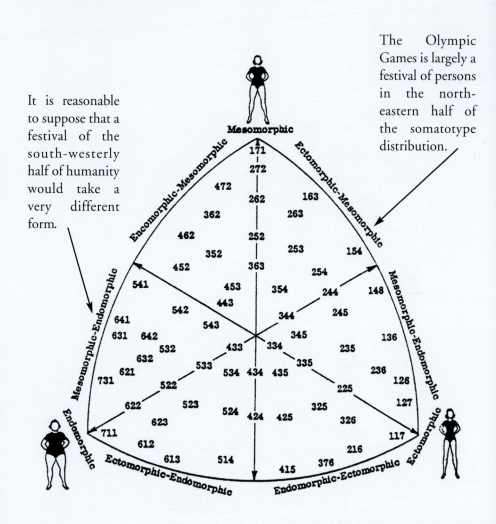

It is reasonable to suppose that a festival of the south-westerly half of humanity would take a very different form.

The Olympic Games is largely a festival of persons in the north-eastern half of the somatotype distribution.

Miracles happen to those who believe in them.

Body Type Questionnaire

The following questionnaire is designed to help you determine which of the three basic body types you conform to. Look at each question and if your body fits then answer:
(a)   score one mark for endomorph,
(b)   one mark for mesomorph,
(c)   one mark for ectomorph.
If you find your body could be equally described by two of the answers to any question then score half a mark for each of them. When you have answered all the questions, add up your marks for each component and this will give you a rough quide to your own body type.

1. How would you describe your body?
    (a)   Rounded
    (b)   Square
    (c)   Long
2. How would you compare the relative sizes of your trunk and the rest of your body?
    (a)   Trunk seems large in relation to the rest of the body
    (b)   They seem well proportioned
    (c)   Trunk seems small in relation to the rest of the body
3. Do you have bulging muscles at any point on your body?
    (a)   No
    (b)   Yes
    (c)   No

Remember that every achievement was once considered impossible.

4. Does your head appear large in relation to your neck?
    (a) No
    (b) No
    (c) Yes
5. Are your bones evident?
    (a) No
    (b) Yes, and they appear large
    (c) Yes, and they appear fine
6. How would you describe your thighs and upper arms?
    (a) Rounded
    (b) Heavily muscled
    (c) Weak
7. Do you have muscular calves and forearms?
    (a) No
    (b) Yes
    (c) No
8. Would you describe your arms as long in relation to your body?
    (a) No, short
    (b) No, about right
    (c) Yes
9. How would you compare your forearms and your upper arms?
    (a) Upper arms are longer than forearms
    (b) Upper arms and forearms the same length
    (c) Forearms longer than upper arms

Things do not change, we change.

10. Are your hands and fingers small in relation to your body?
    (a) Yes
    (b) No, hands and fingers are large
    (c) No, fingers are long but appear fragile
11. Looking at your body from the side, how would you describe your vertebral column?
    (a) Straight
    (b) S-shaped but flat behind the chest
    (c) S-shaped but rounded behind the chest
12. How would you describe your shoulders?
    (a) High, square and with soft contours
    (b) Broad and heavily muscled
    (c) Narrow and rounded
13. How would you describe your hips?
    (a) Broad and soft
    (b) Broad but hard
    (c) Narrow
14. In your trunk does your chest appear more pronounced than your abdomen?
    (a) No, the reverse is so
    (b) Yes, and both appear firm
    (c) Yes, but both appear weak

The way to get ahead - use the one you have.

15. Is the front-to-back measurement of the trunk less than the side-to-side measurement?
    (a) No, they are both equal
    (b) Yes
    (c) Yes, but both are rather small

16. How would you describe your neck?
    (a) Short
    (b) Long and wide
    (c) Long and slender

Now list your marks:
(a).................Endomorph
(b).................Mesomorph
(c).................Ectomorph

For every disciplined effort there is multiple reward.

Is There a Hatha Yoga Body Type?

Is there a body type that is more suitable for performing yoga postures than any other? Well, after a lifetime of looking at people with above average flexibility, it seems to me that these people have a tendency to be below average height and that they are also big boned or mainly mesomorph, around 252 somatotype.

To obtain an accurate somatotype rating would require extensive measurements by experts. However, a rough guide for a person of average height can be found by taking your wrist size; you should measure around the smallest part of your wrist and as close to the bone as possible.

	Ectomorph	*Mesomorph*	*Endomorph*
Male	6.5" (165mm)	7.0" (178mm)	7.5" (190mm)
Female	5.5" (140mm)	6.0" (152mm)	6.5" (165mm)

Racial characteristics as well as body type, play an important part in determining whether you have natural advantages in certain activities. For example, people who live in hot climates tend to have longer limbs than those who come from cooler countries; this is because it helps to cool the body down. Long legs have a distinct advantage in achieving certain yoga postures, like sitting in lotus (Padmasasana). Long arms in relation to the trunk can have big advantages in other yoga postures.

To check your limb length, try the following tests.

Measure a man's wealth by the fewness of his wants.

Arms to height, or 'squaring the man'
1. Lying supine on the floor, heels against a wall, measure the distance between the wall and top of your head.
2. Lying supine, extend arms sideways to push two books outward with finger tips to measure reach, or use a friend to help you.

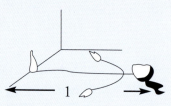 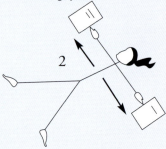

Legs to torso length
1. Sit back against a wall then extend your legs forward. Measure the distance between the back of your pelvis and the soles of your feet.
2. Lying supine, your legs up the wall, measure the distance between the sitting bones and the top of your head.

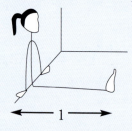 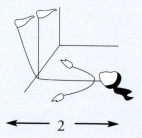

The length of your legs will invariably be longer than your torso and head. If this leg length is substantial it can give you a big advantage in performing certain yoga postures.

To teach someone is to learn twice.

Horses for courses, people for pastimes

Horses perform better on certain racecourses than others. Similarly some people will be able to perform different pastimes much better than others. Why is this? I think it is fairly obvious that no two people are exactly the same. Each individual is unique in their ability to perform activities. This will show up in all areas, like strength, flexibility, balance, coordination, endurance, motivation, etc. Learning where and what your strengths and weaknesses are will give you a much better chance of achieving realistic goals when you set out to learn new skills. Take a look at your own ability in the self-assessment profile below.

Self-Assessment Profile

If I take a truthful look at my motor skills, my all-round ability to coordinate, and the way I generally 'use' myself, I come to the conclusion that, in comparison with some others 'out there':

I AM NOT a fast learner. I AM NOT extremely flexible. I AM NOT prodigiously strong. I AM NOT very well coordinated. I AM NOT all that good at balancing. I AM NOT endowed with vast amounts of stamina. I AM NOT a powerful swimmer, a marathon runner, a fast sprinter, a mountaineer, a skier, a skater, a typist, singer, dancer or actor. In fact, I wonder if I am really above average in any psycho-physical skills at all!

How about YOU?

Do you think you have exceptional talents? If so, why not take a few minutes to assess yourself, honestly? On the next page are a few straightforward and simple areas to consider in assessing your natural ability and possible capabilities.

Man cannot discover new oceans until he has the courage to lose sight of the shore.

Skills	Exceptional	Above average	Average	Below average	Poor or non-attempt
Strength					
Flexibility					
Stamina					
Coordination					
Balance					
Fast learner					
Ball games, (please state)					
Racket sports (please state)					
Any other sports?					
Musical skills (please state)					
Singer					
Dancer					
Other skills?					

By beginning to examine your make-up and psycho-physical ability, you can then use that understanding to consider how you are going to approach your yoga practice and also what degree of success you can expect to achieve. Also has there been any change in your general 'use' as a result of yoga practice? If yes, list some of those changes that you have noticed.

It's a funny thing about life, if you refuse to accept anything but the best you very often get it.

Chapter 4
Flexibility Tests

Some simple, natural flexibility tests (see illustrations in Chapter 2, under ligaments).

Fingers
Bring hands together, then lift palms away as far as you can, leaving fingers still touching.
Palms slightly apart................. Palms apart 45°............... Palms 90°................

Wrists
Hands with palms together in front of your chest, then lift elbows as high as possible and, dropping wrists down, make sure hands stay together.
Arms sloping down............... Arms level................ Arms sloping up...............

Elbow
Straighten one arm against a wall by pressing the palm of your hand on to the wall. Is your arm straight or does it hyperextend?
Arm locked straight.............................. Arm overstraight................................

Thumbs
Try bending your thumb back to touch your forearm, using your other hand to do so.
Thumb close.................. Very close................... Thumb touching..................

It is better to light a candle, than to curse the darkness.

Three Important Flexibility Tests for Hatha Yoga Students

1. Spinal extension (neck)
This test looks at the flexibility of the seven cervical neck vertebrae. This section of the spine gives the freest extension or backward bending movement out of the 24 movable vertebrae in the spine, therefore providing a very good indicator of a person's ability in backward bending postures. You may find a partner helpful for doing this test. Sit down and ask your friend to observe that you only bend back in the neck region and also to check the final position of your face as you do the following test.

Sitting comfortably, with your back upright, use your eyes to follow a line up the wall and along the ceiling. Continue to follow the line with your eyes so that your head moves back into its extreme position. As a rough guide, (a) if your face inclines forward it will indicate tight joints, (b) if the face is level, average joints, (c) if the face inclines backwards, very loose joints.

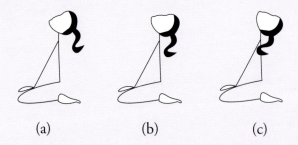

(a)　　　　　　　　(b)　　　　　　　　(c)

Of course, if you have incurred a neck injury or damaged your neck in any way, then the use of this test may be invalid. This would apply to the other tests if the areas indicated have also been damaged.

A man who never makes mistakes never makes anything.

2. Shoulders

Flexibility at the shoulders will give a good indication of a person's ability to perform a number of yoga postures, including many backward bending and arm movements.

To carry out this test you will need a long pole or stick. Hold the pole in front of your body with one hand at the extreme end and the other hand along the pole about three times your shoulders' width apart. Keeping your arms straight throughout the movement, take the pole over your head and down your back, then bring it all the way back to your front. Then move your hands closer together and repeat the movement. Keep this movement going, each time bringing the hands closer together when you return to the starting position.

Continue until you find it impossible to do with straight arms. Then measure the distance between the hands. For the average person this would be approximately two and half times your shoulder width (measure from the outside of the shoulders with arms by your sides). Anyone who registers below one and a half times shoulder width has loose shoulder joints. If you can do this test keeping the hands only shoulder width apart you are possible contortionist material!

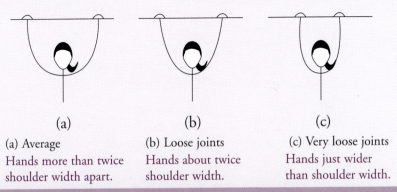

(a) Average
Hands more than twice shoulder width apart.

(b) Loose joints
Hands about twice shoulder width.

(c) Very loose joints
Hands just wider than shoulder width.

The best reformers the world has ever seen are those who commence on themselves.

3. Hamstrings

This particular test is for the 'hamstrings' (biceps femoris, semitendinous, semimembranousus): muscles which run down the back of the upper leg from the sitting bones (ischium) to below the knee joint (upper end of tibia and fibula). This group of muscles works over two joints, the hip and the knee.

Some people have what we call short 'hamstrings', which means they have limited stretch in these three muscles. One of these muscles is called semitendinous – over a third of its length is tendon, which is not designed to stretch.

Beryl Dunn, resident physiotherapist at the Royal Ballet Company for 14 years, says: 'It is virtually impossible to stretch the hamstring muscles and when force is used it is usually the ligaments at the bottom of the back which take the strain.' (Ref 6).

Now with most forward bending, either sitting or standing, the 'hamstrings' are going to be involved. So this group of muscles will very quickly show up an individual's potential and determine whether they are what I call a 'natural forward bender'.

To do this test you need a partner. This is because the person being tested needs to stay relaxed throughout, as this will produce a more accurate assessment. The partner needs to be careful during the testing not to use any more force than is required.

These three tests can be done in a matter of minutes, yet they reveal a great deal about an individual's suppleness.

Study the past if you would divine the future.

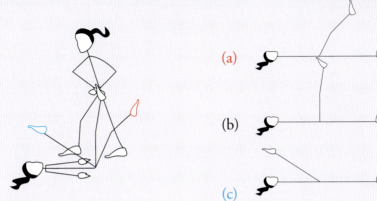

(a)

(b)

(c)

Here is a rough assessment of:
(a) Tight hamstrings, (b) average 90°, (c) loose hamstrings.

Using these three tests it is possible to observe and assess an individual's flexibility, therefore gauging their potential for performing yoga asanas. Flexion and extension, that is forward and backward bending of the human body, is something that you will find in most exercise systems, so these indicator tests could be helpful for those people too.

Once you have actually gauged joint looseness with the neck and the shoulder stick tests, it is quite easy to see how natural looseness affects the full range of movements in all activities, particularly those related to the torso and the upper body.

The 'hamstring' test would indicate the possibility of more stretch and extension in the legs, with greater freedom in the hip joints, giving the individual access to achieving full splits with the legs forward and back, as well as side splits and other variations.

He who can, does. He who cannot, teaches.

Chapter 5
Learning Levels or Plateaus

Learning plateaus occur for just about everyone as they develop new skills. After a period of time, everyone's progress begins to level off. These plateaus may be of a temporary nature but can also become permanent, resulting in no further advancement for that individual. The reasons for this 'lack of progress' could be many and various, for example:

1. Loss of interest.
2. The effort needed to progress is too much for the individual.
3. It is taking up too much of their time.
4. They sense that they have reached their full potential and that's it.

In yoga, as with a great many other skills, I believe that the most noticeable progress will be observed in the first full year of regular practice. By regular practice I mean at least several sessions each week. In fact for the vast majority of people, the most gains are to be observed in the first six months or less. Older students (50+) may not discover their full range of movement potential until after a year or 18 months but on average the first 12 months will show you what is possible as far as asana practice is concerned. This observation is based on frequent and well-structured practice sessions.

In making quicker assessments of an individual's flexibility and potential, we have already looked at some very simple but effective tests in Chapter 4, which can be made before even beginning your yoga practice.

To find yourself, think for yourself.

The Time Factor

In learning a new skill or activity, even with the advantage of natural talent, there remains the all-important consideration of the amount of time you have available for the skill. As we all know, world-class performers in sporting activities spend years of dedication and practice before reaching the top. The same applies to musicians, singers, dancers, etc. They all put in many hours of practice every day and most, if not all of them, begin very early in their life.

This is certainly true with activities that demand peak physical performance, for example Olympic sport stars who devote themselves completely to their sport and also those sports people who only have a short period of time at the top level before retirement. They may also have to give up through injury, possibly due to the intensity of their training. However, the average person 'doing' yoga will not find it easy to keep up a two hours a day, seven days a week practice for years. Most students tend to find that the one and a half or two hour class, once a week, fulfils their needs.

Psychological Effects

It is well understood that exercise will produce chemical changes in the brain and that these changes can have an uplifting effect on the person. So much so that some people can become addicted to exercise systems. They find they have to work out on a regular basis otherwise they feel low and depressed.

However, if your yoga practice is done with control and in a balanced way, you will obtain a sense of well-being and enjoy that feel-good factor with no adverse effects.

Boldness has genius, power and magic in it, begin it now.

Exercise Programme Based on:

1. The fact that the body is made for movement.
2. That the movements should bring about health and vitality.
3. They should not cause pain or strain but maybe some discomfort (see Goswami's four phases of pain)(Ref 7).
4. They should increase or maintain:
   (a) Suppleness, flexibility and relaxation.
   (b) Strength and good muscle tone.
   (c) Endurance.
   (d) Coordination (neuromuscular).
   (e) Sense of balance and natural poise.
   (f) Good respiratory action and cardiovascular activity.
   (g) Symmetrical development.
5. They should be progressive and adaptable to all ages.
6. Be suitable to men and women.
7. Have a holistic approach to body/mind development.
8. Produce confidence, calmness, optimism and a sense of achievement.

Further points to consider for yoga schedules.
9. Competition and the 'end gaining' attitude to be discouraged.
10. Balanced approach between pose/counter-pose and relaxation.
11. Length of time in postures to be determined by students' ability only.
12. Having a well-judged recovery rate. That is sufficient rest between asanas
or pranayama techniques to allow the pulse and respiration to return to normal.
13. Asanas (postures) programme to be completed before pranayama (breathing techniques).
14. Not to make claims for benefits from the postures and breathing techniques, etc., which cannot be substantiated.

Variety's the very spice of life, that gives it all its flavour.

Goswami's Four Phases of Pain

If the posture is neither perfect nor controlled, motionlessness in that posture cannot be attained. The ease stage of a posture is inseparably connected with the physical motionlessness. As soon as the final posture is assumed, the body will be perfectly motionless. If the posture is perfected and controlled, the ease stage will follow immediately. This is the stage most suitable for mental relaxation and concentration. The duration of the ease stage should be gradually increased. Ease stage goes into the discomfort stage when discomfort begins to appear. By regular practice the ease stage is gradually prolonged. Usually the posture is discontinued at the onset of discomfort. The discomfort phase may be subdivided into four phases: discomfort phase, endurance phase, willpower phase and intolerance phase.

When discomfort turns into pain, it is called the pain or endurance phase. If the posture is continued up to this point, the power of toleration of pain is increased and along with it vital endurance is increased. As a result, natural health and natural immunity are established in the body.

The endurance phase should be very carefully and gradually lengthened. However, when pain becomes intense the willpower phase is reached. In bearing the intense pain calmly with the body maintained motionless, will power is called into play and developed to a high level. The willpower phase also should be increased in a systematic manner. At a certain point the intense pain becomes intolerable. At this stage the posture must be discontinued.

Everyone is the architect of his own fortune.

Safety Factors

The class tutor will be looking after external issues that would affect safety, like adequate ventilation, lighting, clean floors, fire exits, etc. They will also need to develop a balanced programme of postures with modifications to cover the variety of different people's abilities and limitations.

However, the greatest safety factor in all exercise systems is the intelligence and understanding of the practitioners to judge their own limits and capabilities. YOU are the No.1 safety factor in your practice. You are the only one who has instant access through your nervous system to know what is happening as you move, so only go as far as your body is telling you at that moment. Never think about what you achieved in your last practice or what you hope to achieve in the future, only focus on what is possible in the here and now.

So the Golden Rule is listen to your own body and do not let anybody force you into a position that you instinctively know is not for you.

Sail while the wind blows: wind and tide wait for no man.

Chapter 6
Competitive Athletic Yogi or Participating Yogi

Most people are 'end-gainers', that is, they seek the end result without giving consideration to the 'means whereby' they gain that 'end'. This competitive conditioning is started at a very early age. At home, for example, we are encouraged to do better than brothers and sisters. At school we work to get to the top of the class and then later to pass exams. Then when we start work, the competitive attitude does not stop. Being successful at business or work means getting to the top. Even when we take time off to play, the object of the exercise is to WIN! So it's not surprising, therefore, that people bring an 'end-gaining' attitude to their pastimes, pursuits and activities, including yoga. Yes, even in yoga practice people are competitive! Trying to get a posture 'right' is a classic example: the end result is the dominating factor. I am not saying that this is a conscious action, on the contrary, most people are convinced that they are not competing with others but they are competing with themselves.

Take a look at the following definition of a competitive athlete, taken from an American publication: 'Competitive athletics has three main connotations: first is that man struggles personally against another person or persons, second that his struggle is impersonally against an objective or external standard, thirdly, that he struggles to better himself, i.e. that he competes with himself. All three of these designations function within the context of Games and Sport. This is consistent with Starr's (1961) definition of competitive athletics as being "a wide range of games and sports, which involve a rivalry or a match with oneself or others".' (Ref. 8).

Words show the wit of man, but actions his meaning.

Competitive athletics thus becomes only a small part of the totality of a person's movement. Physical movement is engaged in for many reasons other than competition and it is here that the main distinction can be made between the athlete and the participant in physical activity. If the performer is competing in the above sense of the word, then he must perforce be regarded as participating in an athletic context. However, if he is simply engaging in physical movement for reasons that do not emanate from his competitive needs or desires, then he can be classified as a participant.

Football players, mountain climbers, golfers, joggers and even dancers, are all athletes, regardless of their ability levels, if their movements are primarily directed towards the pursuit of excellence or success.

Our operational definition of the athlete has now become:
'Any person who executes and completes an identifiable, short-term, skilled motor performance while competing against an objective, external standard, against another person or persons or against oneself.'

I would suggest that most yoga students would find themselves fitting into the above category, as they are trying to compete:

1. Against an external standard, i.e. trying to get the posture right according to a certain book or teacher, etc.
2. Improving their performance (against themselves). How many times have you heard yoga students say, 'Oh, I am getting better at my lotus' or 'I can now do the headstand', etc.'

A rolling stone gathers no moss.

Now of course there is nothing wrong in being a competitive athlete but at least be honest and admit it!

Maintaining the Working Integrity of Yourself

To be a participating yogi, however, is to be striving not to improve performance but to adopt a 'means whereby' approach, which is not striving to get the posture 'right', whatever that means, but to keep looking at what you are doing and trying to see where you may be going wrong. This means that you are shifting the emphasis from the end result to what you have been doing to bring the end result into being. In this process of developing motor skills the main concern must always be to try and maintain your own working integrity. By working integrity we mean all those important functions that are keeping us alive from moment to moment like breathing, circulation, flow of nervous energy, digestion, etc.

The greatest truths are the simplest: so are the greatest men.

10 Observational Feedback Points for the Body in Movement (Yoga Postures)

1. Freedom to breathe easily without strain.

Perhaps the most direct and obvious feedback indicator in movement is, of course, your breath. Before commencing a posture, check your breathing, observe the depth, rhythm and quality of your respiratory action. Then, having moved into a new position, check again, there may be some slight alteration but the basic breathing rhythm and quality should stay the same. If not, then you must have disturbed your own working integrity. Try to remember this: If you don't do yourself any good, then please don't do yourself any harm!

2. Relaxed neck muscles with freely movable head.

Another important way of discovering whether or not your bodily movements or postures are interfering with your general functioning, is to check out your 'head-neck' relationship. Before going into a posture gently move your head from side to side and make a mental note of the range of movement in each direction.

Having gone into the posture, the range of movement should stay the same. In certain postures, i.e. Sarvangasana (shoulder stand), it is not possible to move the head but for most standing and sitting poses you can. This is a very quick and easy action to make and it will immediately show you whether or not you are stiffening your neck muscles. So many people tend to tighten muscles all over their bodies and then expect their bodies to move freely. Try holding this thought in mind: If I stop doing the wrong things, then I may find myself doing the right thing (Ref 9).

He who would gather roses must not fear thorns.

3. Face to be relaxed and free from tension.

It is very important to note that when you observe someone doing a posture you will always look at the body but rarely the face. The reason why you should look at the face is because too many people move the tension out of their bodies into their face, so that their body may move more freely. Then, when they come out of the posture they simple move the tension back into the body. The tension never goes altogether, it simply gets moved about their system. Wilhelm Reich (Ref 10) called this tension 'body armour' and most of us are guilty of hanging on to body armour some of the time.

4. To maintain the working integrity of yourself throughout the movement and in the static position.

What is meant by this is that we do not want to interfere with the general functioning of our organism, that is, breathing, circulation, digestion, flow of nervous energy, etc. - all the things that are keeping you alive from moment to moment. No matter how many specific ends you may gain, you are worse off than before if, in the process of gaining them, you have destroyed the integrity of the organism (Ref 11).

5. To have control over the body's movements at all times.

Here we are considering that as we move from position to position, we should always have the possibility of stopping the movement at any particular stage because we are in control of our bodies. So many people move in an uncontrolled way, allowing their bodies to 'flop' into a posture and also when coming out of it, without thinking what they have done or what they are doing.

6. Avoid excessive tension anywhere.

Again, we are looking for freedom for the body to move easily but so many people get themselves into 'postural sets', that is, they anticipate the movement

Prosperity is located within.

which excites the neuromuscular systems into activity, which creates tension in muscle groups. Then, when it comes to moving, the tension is increased even more, so that we use three or four times more energy than we need.

7. To be aware of joints and muscles involved in the movement.
In this respect we become more consciously aware of what is happening inside the body so that we are familiar with the joints that are being brought into action and the muscles that are being activated in the movement, also in stationary positions, particularly in balancing positions. Here one can become aware of tension in muscle groups very easily. For example, if you try standing on one leg and closing your eyes, you will soon become aware of the muscles which are holding you in the balancing position.

8. Effortless action with minimum use of energy.
When the body is well balanced, the amount of energy required to move it is far less. Learning to retain poise and balance through movements can be acquired through practice.

9. Ability to change habitual manner of use.
It is very important that you do not fall into the trap of always doing things in a habitual way and of not having conscious control over the way in which you use yourself. Occasionally, you should make a deliberate conscious effort to change the way you are doing a posture. For example, say in Matsendrasana (twist pose), if you have always rotated round to the right, then try rotating first round to the left.

10. To be able to repeat the movement again.
In this respect you need to know whether or not the necessary neuromuscular connections have been established satisfactorily, so that you are conscious of the movement and can repeat it again and again whenever you want to.

Often the precious present is wasted in visions of the future.

Chapter 7
Salute to the Sun (Surya Namaskars)

Sun worship has been practised by many people from all over the world from time immemorial. In southern India the ancient Dravidians celebrated the sun's return every morning by performing obeisances or doing exercises. So, the 'sun prayers' can be traced back several thousand years. There are some people who think that these 'sun prayers' predate yoga practice, but because it is all lost in the mists of time I doubt we will ever know for certain. What we do know is that this sequence has been well thought out and provides an excellent all round physical and mental stimulus to start your day.

In modern history the Rajah of Aundh, Shrimant Balasahib Pandit Pratinidhi, brought the 'sun prayers' back into fashion during the 1920s and, although emphasising their ancient and traditional origin, the Rajah improved and adapted them for the 20th century.

Who is the Authority in these Traditional Practices?

As with most yoga practices that have their origins in the distant past, you will come across a number of groups who claim to be the only 'true' followers. They also, as often as not, start running down others who follow a slightly different path. With the 'Salute to the Sun' there are a number of ways the sequence can be interpreted and, because there is no one authority in all this,

A bad beginning makes a bad ending.

each person will adapt and modify their practice according to their own ability and needs. This is perfectly acceptable as long as the purpose and benefits of the practice are maintained.

Aerobic Component in Yoga

In recent years there has been an explosion of interest in yoga but the greatest interest has been towards 'Sashtanga' yoga, or what is sometimes called 'power' yoga, 'fitness' yoga or even 'aerobic' yoga. This lays great stress on dynamic, vigorous and energetic movement producing heat and perspiration in the body. The common theme in all of these systems is the way that the linking movements have been used to produce an aerobic component, something which is not normally seen in yoga practice.

'Sashtanga' Surya Namaskar

The original Sanskrit name of the exercise Sashtanga Surya Namaskar means 'obeisance to the sun with eight points of the body', abbreviated; we call it the Surya Namaskar. The eight points (position 5) are said to relate to touching the ground with head, chest, hands, knees and toes. This is possibly the most significant way of humbling yourself before anyone and certainly to recognising the sun as the giver of life to this planet. So by placing your head and chest on the ground, you bow to the sun with your mind, intellect and thinking, as well as your heart which includes your feelings and emotions.

A moment's insight is sometimes worth a life's experience.

The Salute to the Sun sequence is made up of linking movements which, because of the continuous movement, produce extremely good cardio-vascular activity. Fortunately the 'sun prayers' have an inbuilt adaptability to accommodate most body types and styles and are not just designed for the young and fit.

There are a number of ways that the breathing pattern used in the Salute to the Sun sequence can be interpreted. I am suggesting the following way because it fits into the working integrity and physiology of the body. It is a recognised fact that on the in breath the body tends to be stronger and slightly more rigid, on the out breath it tends to be slightly weaker but more flexible. Which is why when you go to lift a heavy object you naturally breath in deeply and as you lift the object you naturally breathe out, thus avoiding the 'Valsalva Phenomenon' (Ref 12).

As always, with more vigorous action to your body, take the usual precautions. Do not overdo it. Take your time and pay attention to what you are doing, trying to maintain the working integrity of your body as you practise. Far better to do a little practice often, than to try to do too much too soon and end up with aching muscles and stiffness for days after.

You can perform these Surya Namaskars with or without the 'mantra' and can choose how many to perform up to the amount of 24, as long as it is an even number. I would recommend that beginners use the services of an experienced yoga teacher to explain and demonstrate the Salute to the Sun sequence.

Give to the world the best you have and the best will come back to you.

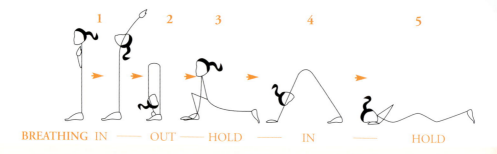

BREATHING IN ——— OUT ——— HOLD ——— IN ——— HOLD

Position 1

Standing upright but relaxed, palms together, thumbs touching the sternum in line with the heart. This salute position (Namaskar) helps to remind you of your individual spirit or 'Atman' residing in the heart centre (Anahata) and you are now dedicating the movements to the universal spirit or 'Brahman'. If you are outdoors in the very early morning you will be facing the rising sun. If indoors you will be facing a 'mandala' or object of your choice, (deity, or picture of your guru, etc.). Standing quite still chant or listen (Ref 13) the mantra 'OM HRAM MITRAYA NAMAH'. Then as you breathe in take both arms down, then lift arms up and above the head, filling the lungs, then as you begin to breathe out, bend gently backwards.

Position 2

Continue breathing out as you pivot through your hip joints, bend forward keeping the spine lengthening and bring the hands to the floor alongside your feet. The lungs are now empty.

Position 3

Step back fully with your left leg, trying to sit down on your right heel, look up, coming into the important 'split' position, keep your lungs empty.

If you don't scale the mountain, you can't see the view.

OUT — IN — OUT — HOLD — IN — RELAXED

Position 4
Then as you breathe in, step back, lift hips up, bring the right leg alongside the left leg, body coming up into an inverted vee position, spine stretched, heels pressed into floor, lungs full.

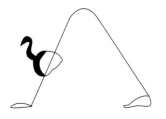

Position 5
Then bending both knees, lower the chest and forehead so that the hands and toes are all touching the floor. This is the humble eight-point position: head and heart touching the ground, lungs full.

Position 6
Breathe out as you arch up and back into 'cobra', giving a good extension position to the spine.

Position 7
Breathe in as you bring your head towards the floor, pushing hard with arms up into the inverted vee position with the lungs full.

Vitality and beauty are gifts of nature for those who live according to its laws.

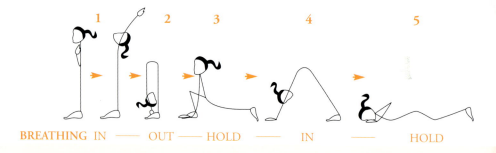

1	2	3	4	5

BREATHING IN —— OUT —— HOLD —— IN —— HOLD

Position 8

Breathe out, stepping forward with left leg, bringing foot between your hands, looking up and arching your back.

Position 9

Lungs empty as you bring right leg forward alongside left, head towards knees in good spinal flexion position.

Position 10

Straighten up as you breathe in back to position 1. Chant the next mantra 'OM HRIM RAVAYE NAMAH' then repeat the sequence, stepping back with the right leg in position 3, coming forward with the right leg in position 8.

A wise man will make more opportunities than he finds.

You need to do two Suyra Namaskars to complete a round. Remember to reverse the leg you take back in position 3 and bring forward in position 8 on the second, fourth, sixth, eighth, tenth and the twelfth sequences.

The important stretching and compression of the spine will give a good stimulation to the spinal cord and the nervous system in general. Also the pressure from the thighs against the ascending and descending colon will encourage peristaltic movement of the intestines, so helping to overcome constipation and allied conditions. Respiratory action will be improved and its long-term effects greatly appreciated, particularly in clearer thinking, better co-ordination and general functioning. You could say that the sequence is one of the finest ways of achieving and maintaining health and well being that has ever been devised.

Nature, to be commanded, must be obeyed.

The Beeja (Bija) Mantras

The beeja mantras are evocative sounds which create vibrations in the body when properly uttered but may or may not have any basic meaning as such. They are not an invocation, or praise of a deity. A mantra has no meaning that can be grasped by the mind and the intellect.

The mantras used in Surya Namaskars are kindly, beneficent, happy, joyous ones. Use them without any reserve or fear.
Pranava Aum or 'OM' comprises: A = Vishnu, U = Shiva and M = Brahman. Aum or 'OM' ryhmes with *home*.

The beeja mantras are:
aum ... *hram* (rhymes with *calm*)   *aum* ... *hreem* (rhymes with *seem*)
aum ... *hroom* (rhymes with *room*)   *aum* ... *hraim* (rhymes with *time*)
aum ... *hraum* (rhymes with *round*)   *aum* ... *hrah* (rhymes with *hurrah*)

In these basic beeja mantras almost all the possible vibrations of an individual are included. You will notice that there are six beeja mantras and 12 names for the sun, so to complete the 12 Namaskars the beeja mantras are repeated.

The 12 movements provide one of the best all-round workouts for the body and, when complemented by the mantra the whole sequence develops meaning, purpose, and a sense of timing, which is why many students find its practice first thing in the morning so rewarding.

For the purpose of this book I am only recommending 12 movements. More can be performed but this will be at the discretion of the student or teacher.

We grow only when we push ourselves beyond what we already know.

The beeja mantras are chanted at the commencement of each sequence. The mantra associated with the sequence provides not only a spiritual connotation but also gives purpose and meaning to the actions. The mantra gives one a sense of timing which is so important when one is practising alone. Before you start check that you have sufficient room behind you to step back and also remember to alternate the leg which steps back each time.

Make sure that you fit the movements into your breathing rhythm and then you will be working in harmony with yourself.

Here are the 12 names of the sun with the beeja mantras:

1. Aum Hram Mitraya (Friend of all) Namah
2. Aum Hreem Ravaye (Praised by all) Namah
3. Aum Hroom Suryaya (Guide of all) Namah
4. Aum Hraim Bhanave (Bestower of beauty) Namah
5. Aum Hraum Khagaya (Stimulator of the senses) Namah
6. Aum Hrah Pushne (Nourisher of life) Namah
7. Aum Hram Hiranyagarbhaya (Promoter of virility) Namah
8. Aum Hreem Marichaye (Destroyer of disease) Namah
9. Aum Hroom Adityaya (Inspirer of love) Namah
10. Aum Hraim Savitre (Begetter of life) Namah
11. Aum Hraum Arkaya (Inspirer of awe) Namah
12. Aum Hrah Bhaskaraya (Refulgent one) Namah

Knowledge itself is power.

Loosening Exercises for Surya Namaskar

Here are some loosening exercises which have proved to be useful to students over a number of years. They will help you to stretch muscles and to open up joints. These exercises can be used for general loosening purposes in all types of posture.

First of all, the important split position from the Salute to the Sun. If you get this part right then you will find the rest of the sequence tends to fall into place quite easily. It's the one part which most people have difficulty with. From the standing position step forward with the right leg and step back with your left. Bring the hands down alongside your front foot, try to sit down on the forward heel and stretching your left leg back, keep your back straight and look forward. Relax the breathing in this position.

Now, as you breathe in step back with your right leg and bring the right foot alongside your left. Press both heels hard down into the floor, also try to bring the head down to the floor, this will stretch the spine and also stretch the backs of your legs so that the body is in the inverted vee position. As you breathe out step forward with your left leg, bring the left foot right up between the hands, look forward and keep your back straight now and on the next in breath, step back with the left leg, bring the feet together and press the heels down once more stretching the backs of your legs. Try to press your head down between your arms giving your spine a very good stretch. Continue to do this movement alternately, stepping back, bringing the feet together, pushing the heels down hard into the floor, getting an intense stretch through your legs and your back.

When you have faults, do not fear to abandon them.

Leg Stretches

Lower leg stretch
Start by kneeling down, then take right foot forward, forming a box shape, right shin and left thigh vertical. Then bring both hands on to your right knee. On the out breath allow the right knee to go forward, making sure your right heel stays on the floor. Keep the breathing relaxed but on each out breath encourage the knee further forward over the toes. Now as the muscles tighten up in your legs, you have to 'talk' to your muscles. Just ask them to relax, remember a muscle will stretch when it releases, so be patient with yourself once the muscles have relaxed and they will be capable of lengthening. Then you can take your knee further forward over your toes.

Repeat this procedure with your left leg forward.

This action will improve the flexibility of the ankle joints and stretch the calf muscles. Another important muscle group that requires stretching is the iliopsoas. To accomplish this, the following psoas stretch exercise is excellent.

The reward of a thing well done is to have done it.

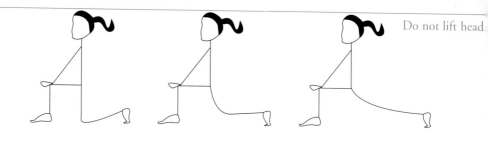

Do not lift head

Psoas stretch

Again commence by kneeling down, then take the right foot forward, forming box shape, right shin and left thigh vertical. Tuck the toes of the left foot under and step forward your foot length with the right foot, placing your heel where your right toes were, breathing relaxed.

Lift the left knee up off the floor, so that you balance on your right foot and your left toes. Maintain this balanced state with relaxed breathing. Now without lifting your head and trunk, straighten your back leg, pushing your left heel away.

This will give an intense stretch through your left leg, particularly to inner thigh and groin area. Hold this position for approximately 15–20 seconds, then lower left knee to floor, and relax.

Repeat this movement twice more, holding for 15–20 seconds, then relaxing completely.

Now reverse the position of the legs. Left leg forward and right leg back, toes tucked under, step forward your foot length, lift the right knee up and balance on your left foot and right toes, relaxed breathing. Again stretch right heel back, straightening right leg without lifting head or torso higher, hold for 15–20 seconds, then release right back knee to the floor and repeat three times. Then rest. Keep breathing relaxed throughout these stretches, emphasising maximum stretch always during the out breath.

We learn wisdom from failure much more than from success.

Cobra - Dog Stretch

Now for the important forward and backward bending positions, sometimes referred to as 'down and up facing dog pose', or just simple raised cobra and dog poses. Start by bringing the hands on to the floor, shoulder width apart, fingers facing forward, feet hip width apart, toes facing forward. Adopting the inverted vee position, try to keep the heels in contact with the floor.

In this position breathe out fully through the mouth in a series of 'whooshes' whilst at the same time trying to increase the stretch through the back and down the back of the legs. Then as you breathe in through the nostrils, take the body through the arms and into the raised cobra position, with the lungs filled. Again 'whoosh' the air out through the mouth at the same time, trying to arch back strongly each time, thereby intensifying the extension of the spine. Then as you breathe in, come up into the 'dog' or inverted vee position, pushing the hips up high, stretching the backs of your legs and pressing the heels down hard into the floor. Again 'whoosh' the air out, then as you breathe in, swing back into the raised cobra position. Continue with this alternating cobra-dog movement for a number of times or until fatigue stops you.

This will help to make the Surya Namaskar positions a great deal easier.

Don't just dream it, do it.

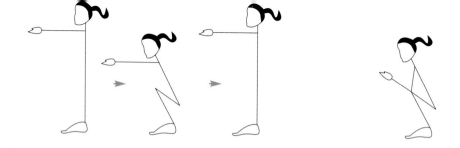

The Importance of the Squat

The lack of mobility in the hips amongst most western people is pretty well recognised. This creates many problems, some of which can be corrected by working on the flat-footed squats.

So, place your feet slightly wider than your hips, then check where your toes are pointing because when you bend your knees they must go over the toes. This means that you will be working the knee joint through its line, thereby avoiding injuries.

Now, as you breathe in lift both arms forward and up to shoulder height. Then, as you breathe out release the knees forward and keeping the head, neck and trunk in a straight line sink into a deep flat-footed squat, making sure your heels stay in contact with the floor. As you breathe in come back up to standing, breathe out and lower your arms. Repeat this movement ten times, then rest. To make this more difficult you can take the feet further apart each time, till you reach an optimum position. Then to move the feet back, this will work the muscles from a slightly different angle each time. The next challenge is to bring the feet closer together each time, seeing if you can squat with the feet touching.

After you have done this, try to remember the position where your feet felt most comfortable, take them to that position now and go into a squat. Now bring your elbows against the knees and gently push outward with knees pushing inwards, relax the breathing whilst you do this. Stay in this position for about ten breaths. You will notice the effect of this when you straighten up.

We are what we repeatedly do;
excellence, then, is not an act but a habit.

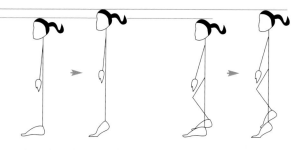

Heel Raising and the 'Soleus Pump'

Now for some heel raising. Stand with the feet slightly apart, come up on to the toes, breathing relaxed, rock back on to the heels, come up on to the toes, back onto the heels and continue with this rocking movement, getting a nice rhythm going. Keep this movement going but as you come back on to the heels move the toes out to a 45º angle and do several heel raises. Then move the feet out further almost at right angles to each other and continue rocking up on to the toes and down onto the heels. Then turn the feet out as far as is possible for you, do several more heel raises then stop and give your legs a thorough shake to take away any tightness or discomfort. Then bring the feet together, turn the heels out and toes in, this will feel very strange and awkward at first, then do a few more heel raises. This will work the muscles from a different angle and you may feel the effect on the outside edge of the calf muscle.

If you have very powerful calf muscles you can always make them work to maximum by doing heel raising on one leg, with the other foot behind the heel of the leg you are working.

As you know, the blood returning to the heart from the legs is not under arterial pressure, it comes back through the veins which run through muscles. When the leg muscles contract they squeeze the blood through non-return valves. Because the lower leg is a long way from the heart, blood tends to 'pool' and there is very little activity. By contracting the deep lying soleus muscle, you are encouraging the venous return and improving circulation.

If you fail to plan, you plan to fail.

Brief Summary

It seems that **natural flexibility** has a great deal to do with your individual body type and is, therefore, determined at birth.

Females tend to be more flexible than males but there will always be exceptions.

Some **racial characteristics** appear to make certain postures easier, for example, long limbs and lotus (Padmasana).

The **age** when practice begins has a large influence on the level of achievement that is possible.

The **amount of time** available to practise will also be a strong factor in determining progress.

Motivation and the will to progress are possibly the number one reasons why people succeed or fail in mastering many difficult skills and activities.

It seems that the ability to perform certain Hatha yoga postures may be determined by your genes but the ultimate goal of yoga, that of self-realisation, is open to all.

*What lies behind us and what lies before us
are tiny matters compared to what lies within us.*

References

1. *Hatha Yoga (The report of a personal experience)* by Theos Bernard, Rider & Co., 1950.
2. *How to Know God (The Yoga Aphorism of Patanjali).* Trans. by Swami Pradhavananda and Christopher Isherwood. Patanjali was the first person to put yoga down in writing, the date of these Yoga sutras it has been suggested could vary between 4th century B.C. and 4th century A.D.
3. Jiddu Krishnamurti. 1895–1986.
4. *The Concise Oxford Dictionary*, University Press, Oxford.
5. W.H.Sheldon, *The Atlas of Man* and *Varieties in Human Physique*, Harper, New York, 1940.
6. Beryl Dunn, *Dance! Therapy for Dancers*, Heinemann Health Books, 1974.
7. Extract from: Chapter 7 *Hatha Yoga* by Professor Shyam Sundar Goswami, L.N. Fowler & Co., Ltd., 1959.
8. R.A. Alderman *Psychological Behaviour in Sport.*
9. Chapter 1. Evolution of a Technique, F. M. Alexander, *The Use of the Self,* Victor Gollancz, London, 1985.
10. Wilhelm Reich, *The Sexual Revolution* & *Character Analysis*, Vision Press.
11. Chapter 1, Escape from the Monkey Trap, *Freedom to Change,* F. P. Jones.
12. Valsalva Phenomenon, holding the breath when lifting heavy objects, elevates systolic blood pressure and causes other effects to the heart which could cause the individual to lose consciousness!
    Science of Stretching by Michael J. Alter
    Human Kinetics Books, 1988.
13. Hatha Yoga Practice tape (90 minutes by Ken Thompson) or Surya Namaskar Salute to the Sun Sequence CD. Both of these include the authentic Bija Mantra chants performed by Pandit Vishnu Narayan; sanskrit scholar, hindu priest and yoga expert.
    These items can be purchased from Angela's Books, 65 Norfolk Road, Seven Kings, Ilford, Essex IG3 8LJ. Please send for a free catalogue, or email: ken_thompson@lineone.net.

He has enough who is content.

Bibliography

F. M. Alexander, *The Use of The Self*, Victor Gollancz, London, 1985.

R. A. Alderman, *Psychological Behaviour in Sport*, Thomson Learning, 1974.

M. J. Alter, *Science of Stretching*, Human Kinetics Books, 1988.

Theos Bernard, *Hatha Yoga*, Rider & Co, 1950.

Beryl Dunn, *Dance! Therapy for Dancers*, Heinemann Health Books, 1974.

P.M. Galley & A.L. Forster, *Human Movement*, Churchill Livingstone, 1982.

Professor S. S. Goswami, *Hatha Yoga*, L.N. Fowler, 1959.

Frank Pierce Jones, *Freedom to Change*, Mouritz, London, 1997.

Apa Pant, *Surya Namaskar*, Orient Longman, 1970.

Principles of Anatomy and Physiology for Physical Training Instructors in the RAF, HMSO, 1959.

C. Isherwood, *Swami Pradhavananda How to Know God*, Signet Books, 1959.

Shritmant Balasahib & Pandit Pratinidhi, *The Ten Point Way to Health*, J.M. Dent, 1938.

Wilhelm Reich , *The Sexual Revolution & Character Analysis*, Vison Press, 1951.

W.H. Sheldon, *The Atlas of Man & Varieties in Human Physique*, Harper, New York, 1940.

*Nature is often hidden,
sometimes overcome, seldom extinguished.*

Index

Age	11
Asanas	13, 45, 47, 49, 50
Matsendrasana	58
Padmasasana	37, 54, 75
Sarvangasana	56
Ball and socket joint	20, 21
Beeja (bija) mantras	66, 67
Brain	17
Breathing	12, 49, 56, 61
Calf muscles	69, 73
Cobra posture	63, 71
Competitiveness	53-55
Condyloid joint	21
Disability	11
Discomfort phase	50
Dog stretch	71
Ectomorph	31-33, 36, 37
Elbow joint	21, 23, 24, 41
Endomorph	22, 31-33, 36, 37
Face	17, 57
Fingers	22, 25, 26, 41
Gliding joint	21
Golgi tendon organ (GTO)	27, 28
Goswami's four phases of pain	49, 50
Hamstrings	44, 45
Headstand	54
Hinge joint	21
Hip joint	20, 21, 25, 44, 45, 72
Homeostasis	29

Riches are for spending.

Joints	20-25, 28, 30, 41-45, 58, 68, 69
Ball and socket	20, 21
Condyloid	21
Elbow	21, 23, 24, 41
Gliding	21
Hinge	21
Hip	20, 21, 25, 44, 45, 72
Knee	21, 25, 44, 72
Pivot	21
Saddle	21
Shoulder	20, 21, 43
Knee joint	21, 25, 44, 72
Ligaments	15, 16, 20-22, 25, 44
Lotus posture	37, 54, 75
Mantras	62, 66, 67
Matsendrasana	58
Mesomorph	22, 31-33, 36, 37
Muscles	15, 16, 24-29, 31, 58, 68, 69
Calf muscles	69, 73
Muscle memory	17
Muscle spindles	26, 27
Rectus abdominous muscle	16
Natural ability	19, 48
Neck	42, 56
Nervous system	15, 17
Overdoing	15, 17, 25, 61
Padmasasana	37, 54, 75
Pain	50
Pivot joint	21
Postures	13, 20, 49, 50
Cobra	63, 71
Dog	71

Think all you speak, but speak not all you think.

Headstand	54
Lotus	37, 54, 75
Shoulder stand	56
Twist	58
Pranayama	12, 49, 56, 61
Proprioceptive neuromuscular facilitating	28
Psoas stretch	69, 70
Rectus abdominous muscle	16
Saddle joint	21
Safety	51
Salute to the Sun	59-68
Sarvangasana	56
Sashtanga yoga	60
Sex (gender)	11, 20
Shoulder joint	20, 21, 43
Shoulder stand	56
Soleus pump	73
Somatotype	22, 31-33, 36, 37
Spinal extension	42
Spine	16, 22, 29
Squat	72
Stretches	
Dog stretch	71
Psoas stretch	69, 70
Sun prayers	59-68
Surya Namaskars	59-68
Tendons	15, 25-27
Thumb	21, 23, 41
Twist pose	58
Valsalva Phenomenon	61
Wrist joint	41

Knowing others is wisdom,
knowing the self is enlightenment.